# MAGICAL CHANGO

An Enchanting Story Of Manners And Friendship

By

Diana Lewis

Illustrated by Katherine Rose Slocum

ISBN: 0-9659901-3-3

Published by:

DiLee Publications
P.O. Box 623
Manhattan, Montana
59741

To order additional copies of Magical Chango, send check or money order for $9.95 plus $2.00 Postage and Handling to the above address.

All copies will be autographed.

Publishing Consultant: Jeri D. Widmer

Foreword

Ever notice a child misbehaving and think to yourself, doesn't anyone teach manners anymore? Whether you are a teacher, a grandparent or a parent it's time to read this enchanting story of manners and friendship to the little ones.

For years there has been a void in the children's book industry on books that deal with manners for small children. MAGICAL CHANGO teaches manners with love and understanding to young children. This story by Diana Lewis, with the help of her friend Chango (a magical stuffed monkey), leads a young girl through a series of short and easily understood lessons in day to day manners in order to attract and keep friends. As the story unfolds the child learns it's just as important to be a friend to yourself as well as others, through manners.

Hopefully most children know the basics of please and thank you by the time they enter school. This fun book goes a little deeper. Respecting your family and teachers, responsibility, cleanliness, sharing, being thoughtful and more are all covered by Magical Chango, whose voice can only be heard by the children in their WISH IMAGINATION.

Printed by: Color World Printers, Bozeman, Montana USA

# MAGICAL CHANGO

It was a beautiful day in San Diego for Maria's fifth birthday party. "I hope the people that come to my party bring me lots of big, expensive gifts." Maria thought as she watched the children arrive all wishing her Happy Birthday. Just then Maria noticed her Grandmother arriving carrying a large box. Maria got so excited she pushed past her guests and took the large box out of Grandmother's arms without even saying "hello" or "I missed you Grandmother." Even though Maria had not seen her Grandmother for a long time, Grandmother lives in a small village in Mexico.

Grandmother knelt down next to Maria as she tore into the gift. Grandmother said "Maria, I told an old friend in our village that I was coming to California to wish you a Happy Birthday and she made this little stuffed monkey for you. My friend said that his name is Chango and he has special powers." As Maria held Chango high above her head she whined, "I don't want another stuffed animal, if you have special powers why don't you turn yourself into a golden necklace?"

As Grandmother watched Maria's bad manners her thoughts went back many years to the time when she was raising her own famalia in Mexico. How we cherished the moments we could all spend together, caring, teaching and loving each other, somehow life today seems to be too busy for teaching manners and kindness.

As if by magic Grandmother could hear her own mother's voice saying "Amigas come and go but famalias are always here for us." These thoughts suddenly made Grandmother sad for Maria and yet she knew that Maria's Mother was working very hard to raise her little girl by herself, she needed help!

Suddenly Grandmother felt the magic in Chango's heart and knew Chango would help Maria become the charming, loving child that Grandmother wished for. Grandmother thought, if I could make a wish of Chango's special powers, I would wish Chango could somehow teach my beautiful Maria charm and manners, because beauty comes from within as well as physically. Maria would even like herself, she thought.

After Maria had torn open the other gifts, not once saying "Thank You" to her guests, the party moved into the dining room for cake and ice cream. Chango sadly noticed Maria licking her fingers, talking while chewing, eating fast and noisily, and paying no attention at all to her guests. After watching Maria, Chango knew why Grandmother had made such a wish. I will teach Maria all about manners and getting along with people, Chango thought.

Maria had ice cream and cake all over her face and dress and even some on the floor, when she heard. "Wash your face and hands and clean up the mess you made on the chair and floor." Maria turned to look in the direction of the voice but there was no one there except the stuffed monkey that Grandmother had given her. Again she heard the voice "If you make a mess, you must clean it up, then you will learn it is easier to be more careful." "My Mother will clean the mess up!" Maria said in a loud voice, not realizing no one else in the room had heard Chango.

"Did you say something Maria?" asked her Mother. "Yes, I told that monkey that you would clean up my mess." replied Maria. "Why are you talking to that monkey?" asked her Mother. "Because he is talking to me." said Maria. Maria's Mother went about cleaning up after the party mess with a somewhat puzzled look on her face. I wish Maria were more considerate of others, thought her Mother. Maria's Mother was trying her best to raise Maria by herself, but she had to work and that left little time to spend with Maria, the precious time she and Maria both wanted and needed.

Later as Maria lay down to take a nap she again heard the voice. “Maria, let me introduce myself, my name is Chango and I was made by my amiga, Packy, she lives in Kino Bay, Mexico.” Maria sat up in bed, she couldn’t believe her eyes or ears for there sat Chango in his box smiling. In the beginning she was frightened but soon saw and felt the warmth and love in Chango’s heart and wanted to hear him speak again.

“What does amiga mean?” asked Maria. Chango smiled and said “Amiga means friend in Spanish the spoken language of your heritage.” Chango continued “As each day passes, you will find that friends are a very important part of your happiness and you will bring happiness to others too, but first you must learn to like yourself, to be your OWN BEST FRIEND and manners are a good way to start.” “What are manners?” asked Maria. “I am glad you asked,” Chango said “because the reason I was chosen by your Grandmother is to tell you about manners.” Chango sat up a little taller in his box and continued. “Manners are the polite things people do for each other. Being polite and nice makes getting along with each other pleasant.” Maria said, “Tell me more about manners Chango, because I want to have friends, sometimes I don’t think anyone likes me.” Chango seemed pleased that Maria was so interested, “First you must be a friend to have a friend.” replied Chango.

Chango began to tell Maria about all the different kinds of manners that all children should have.

Chango said "Picking up your shoes, toys and clothes from the floor and wiping your feet when they are muddy. This is called

NEATNESS

Keeping your body clean, washing your hair and ears, brushing your teeth and wearing clean clothes.  This is called

CLEANLINESS

When you sneeze put your hand over your mouth so you won't spread germs to others and when passing a person always pass behind them. When you borrow something, always return the item. There is also a time to be quiet, when family or teachers are reading, or speaking. This is called

COURTESY

Sharing your toys and cookies, not always taking the last cookie on the plate or the biggest or not laughing when someone falls or gets hurt. This is called

GENEROSITY

Respecting other people and the things that belong to them, and respecting other people's ideas, even if you don't agree with them. When you have friends over, or are a visitor in someone's home, be on your best behavior and make everyone feel comfortable and welcome. Don't interrupt or complain. This is called

CONSIDERATION

When playing games never cheat or lie, play fairly and you will enjoy the game more. You get nothing from cheating or lying except a bad feeling in your heart. This is called

HONESTY

When you are told that it is time for bed or study or “No, you can’t have more candy or cake” don’t argue, listen to them, they have very good reasons for not letting you do some things. This is called

OBEDIENCE

Pets need love and care too.  Don't forget to feed your pets and give them lots of hugs.  This is called

RESPONSIBILITY

You must try very hard to get along with people, especially your family, to earn their respect and friendship. This is called

LOVE

Maria, if you learn all of these manners, you will then have charm, which will give you special powers throughout your life. People will want to be your friend. You see Maria, life is a little like making a quilt. God makes the design and it is up to each of us to create the colors as we go through life. Yes, we all make mistakes but when we look back over our quilt, how nice to say to ourselves "That is the most beautiful quilt I have ever seen."

Just then the door to Maria's room opened and Mom said "Maria, please go to sleep, you have had a very busy day." "Yes Mother," Maria said. "Oh Mother, thank you for a wonderful birthday party and tomorrow I will tell everyone thank you for coming to my party."

Maria's Mother looked surprised at her daughter's thoughtfulness, as she bent down to kiss her, she said softly, "Happy Birthday Maria, I love you so much, you are very special to me."

Drifting off to sleep and feeling very special and loved, Maria looked deep into Chango's eyes and said "I am glad you are my friend, sometimes when my Mom is at work I feel frightened and scared, but now I can talk to you anytime I want, because you are my amiga."

Chango gently smiled and said "I have lots of special powers, all you have to do is have a WISH IMAGINATION and I can grow as tall as your apartment building to protect you or as small as a penny so you can take me with you anywhere. I'll always be here for you, my special Maria."

Maria didn't hear Chango, she was asleep. "We have the rest of our lives together to learn manners and "WISH IMAGINATION." Chango thought as he too drifted off to sleep.

PHOTO BY JERI WIDMER

# ABOUT THE AUTHOR

## DIANA LEWIS

Fifteen years ago I fell in love with a tall Montana man, married and moved my young children from Virginia to Bozeman, Montana. The best decision I have ever made! However, in the process we both inherited each other's children, needless to say it was interesting, which prompted me to write this book shortly after we married.

As most teachers, parents and grandparents are aware, it can be difficult to teach or discipline another's child, particularly if you happen to be a STEP-parent or STEP-grandparent. With that in mind I decided it would be easier to teach my new grandchildren manners through a Magical Monkey named Chango.

Recently while viewing the Oprah show on forging ahead with projects lying around on the shelf, with the encouragement of my husband Lee, six grown children and five grandchildren, I decided it was time to dust off my book and share it with you!

Lee and I live in the Gallatin Valley, near Bozeman, Montana, where we have raised our family in full view of the mountains and under the Big Sky and are enjoying every minute of our lives together. Meanwhile I am busy working on Chango's next adventure which deals with small children's fears.